CW00665241

JOHN THOMPSON'S
EASIEST PIANO COURSE

PART FOUR

PLAYBACK+

Speed • Pitch • Balance • Loop

To access audio, visit:
www.halleonard.com/mylibrary

"Enter Code"
6880-7275-4432-1140

Design, Illustration and Typesetting by Xheight Limited
Barnett, England

ISBN 978-1-4950-2347-7

WILLIS MUSIC

EXCLUSIVELY DISTRIBUTED BY

HAL•LEONARD®

7777 W. BLUEMOUND RD. P.O. BOX 13819
MILWAUKEE, WISCONSIN 53213

Teachers and Parents

The primary purpose of PART FOUR is to allow the student the opportunity to develop efficiency and fluency in the application of knowledge gained in the earlier books. For that reason, there are not many new demands made in a technical way.

Several new keys are introduced, namely E Major, B Major, A Flat Major, D Flat Major and G Flat Major. The examples in the new keys are purposely kept simple. Leger lines between the staves are also presented with charts showing an easy way to recognize notes written on the added lines. The dotted quarter note is explained and examples given in three-four and four-four time. There are also examples in which a change of fingers is required when playing repeated notes. This, of course, results in an extension of hand position and prepares the way for passing the thumb under and the hand over, a phase of technique taken up in Part Five. Simple use of the pedal is allowed in some of the later pieces and it prepares the student for detailed study of the art of pedalling which is also taken up in Part Five.

So PART FOUR, except for the points outlined above, is mostly a book of review work. It should afford the student a chance to enjoy the fruits of his/her labor to date, and at the same time develop better technique, musicianship and general musical understanding.

When this book is finished, the student will be ready for another advance in technique and the following book will contain material with more extended passage playing. Meanwhile, every effort should be made to play the examples in this book with the best possible artistry.

John Thompson

Contents

Wrist Staccato
Dancing Raindrops

TEACHER'S NOTE: This number should be played with a bouncing wrist staccato. For development of the various touches, use John Thompson's HANON STUDIES, specially designed for use at this level.

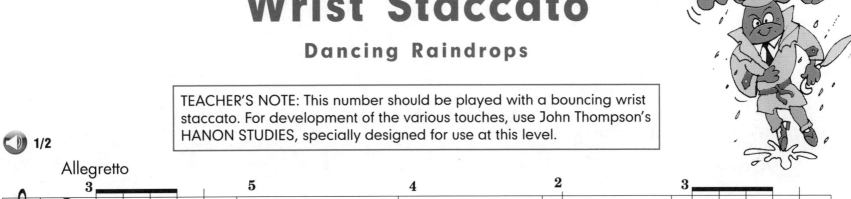

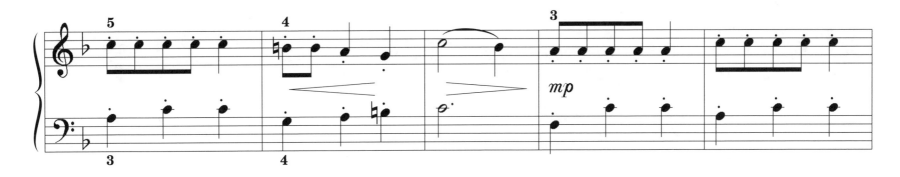

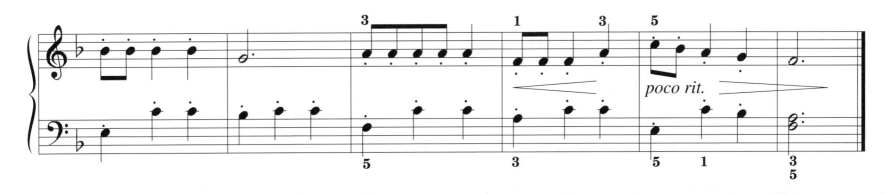

6

Melody in the Left Hand

At the Ball

In this piece the melody lies in the left hand. Try to play it with your best singing tone while the right hand supplies a light staccato accompaniment of familiar chord patterns learned earlier in the course.

3/4

Allegretto

8

Leger Lines
(Above the bass staff)

Leger lines are little lines added above or below the staff upon which to write additional notes. The leger lines **above** the bass staff are easy to read if it is remembered that all lines **above Middle C** are really treble lines, **borrowed and brought down** for use as leger lines.

Example:

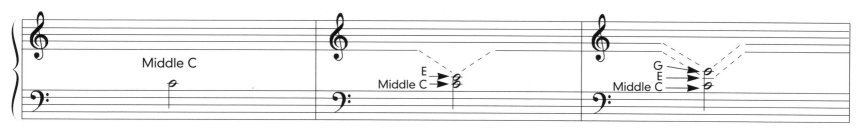

1st line of the treble brought down to become E in the bass.

2nd line of the treble brought down to become G in the bass.

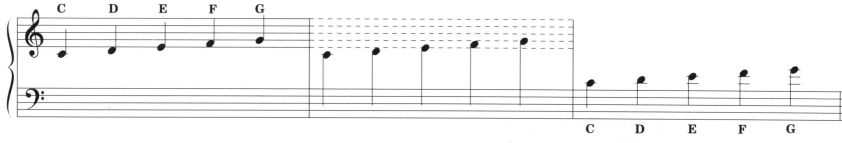

These notes in treble clef

– when transposed to bass clef

– look like this on the music.

Writing Exercises

Write the letter-names under these notes, then transpose them to treble clef.

Transpose these notes to the bass clef, using leger lines.

Etude on Leger Lines

Remember that all added lines **above** Middle C are **borrowed** from the treble and brought down as leger lines.

5/6

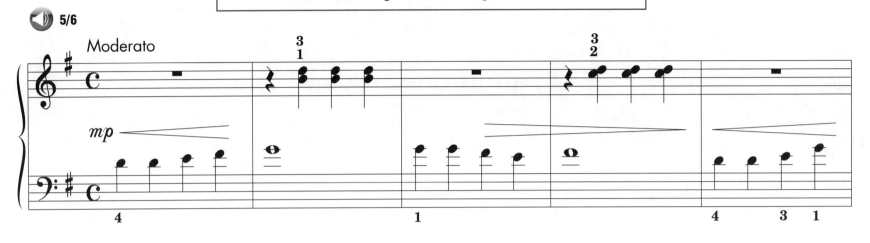

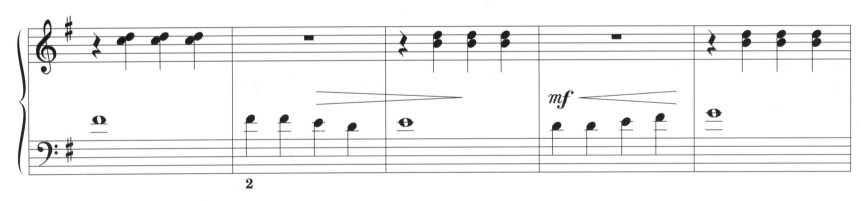

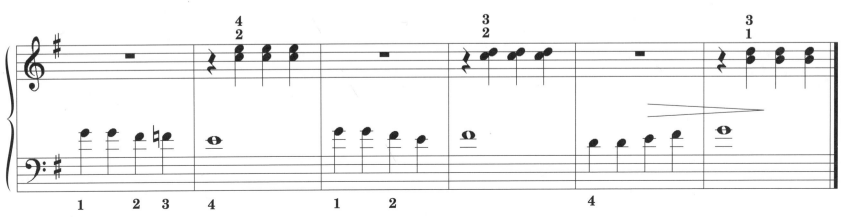

Dotted Quarter Notes (In Three-Four)

You have already played dotted half notes and learned how the dot adds an extra **half value** to each note marked.
A dotted quarter note is equal to one full count plus one half of the next count. If you imagine a tie connecting the full count to the next half count, it will be easy to play.

Example:
written   played

7/8

Song of the Brook

Dotted Quarter Notes (In Four-Four)

Puck

9/10

Played

Apply extra emphasis or stress to all notes marked with the accent sign > or >

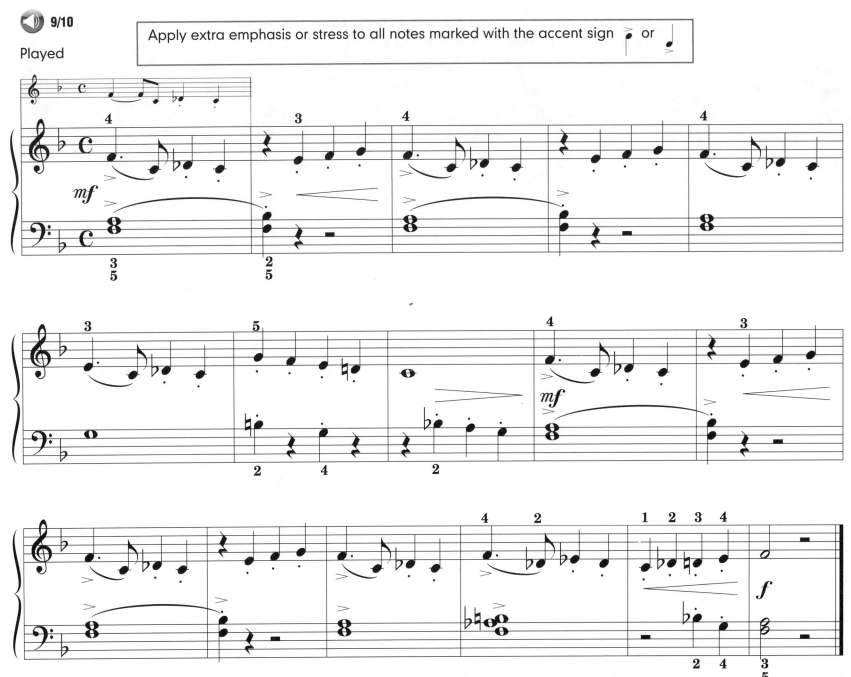

Leger Lines
(Below the Treble Staff)

The leger lines **below** the treble staff are easy to read if it is remembered that all lines **below Middle C** are really bass lines, **borrowed and brought up** for use as leger lines.

Example:

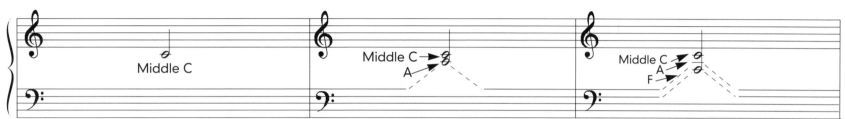

1st line of the bass brought up to become A in the treble.

2nd line of the bass brought up to become F in the treble.

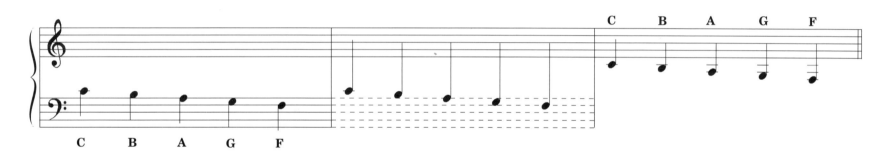

These notes in bass clef — when transposed to treble clef — look like this on the music.

Writing Exercises

Write the letter-names over these notes, then transpose them to bass clef.

Transpose these notes to the treble clef, using leger lines.

Remember that all added lines **below** Middle C are bass lines, **borrowed** and used as leger lines in the treble.

Finger Change on the Same Key

From a Story Book

A change of fingers when a key is repeated results automatically in a new hand position, thus increasing the number of keys lying within reach of the fingers. Watch the fingering carefully in the following piece.

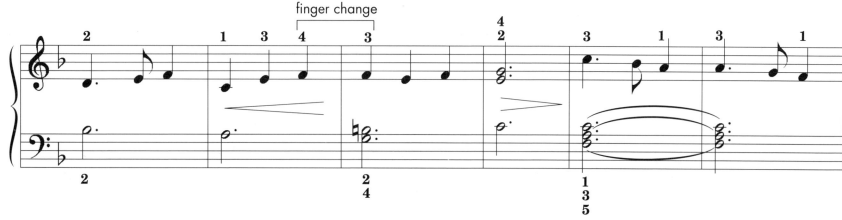

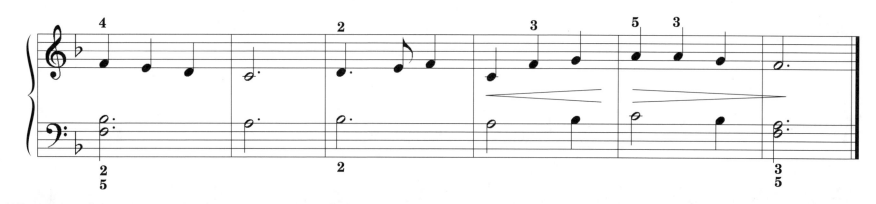

Comin' 'Round the Mountain

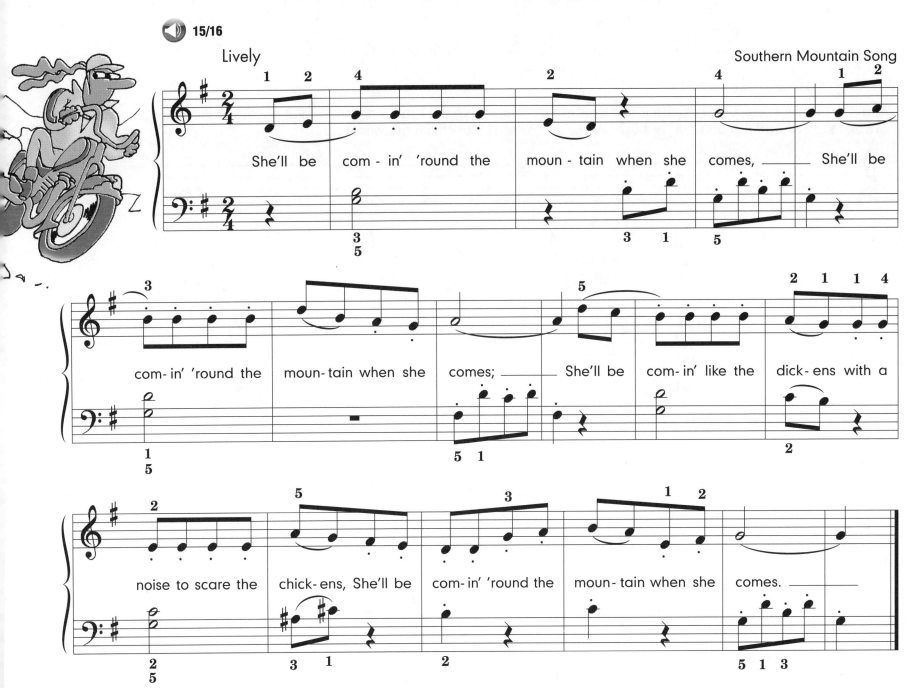

Lively

Southern Mountain Song

15/16

She'll be com-in' 'round the moun-tain when she comes, _____ She'll be

com-in' 'round the moun-tain when she comes; _____ She'll be com-in' like the dick-ens with a

noise to scare the chick-ens, She'll be com-in' 'round the moun-tain when she comes. _____

Watch carefully for the finger changes in the above piece.

Work Sheet New Key – E Major

E MAJOR has four sharps – F♯ C♯ G♯ D♯.

Write the E major scale, using accidentals as necessary to preserve the scale pattern. Remember that half steps occur only between the **3rd and 4th** and **7th and 8th** degrees of the scale. All others are whole steps.

The E major signature looks like this.

Copy it here.

Write the E major triad in this form:

Five-Finger Exercise in E Major

Dancing Fingers

Be sure to make a distinction between the slurred groups and staccato notes in this piece.

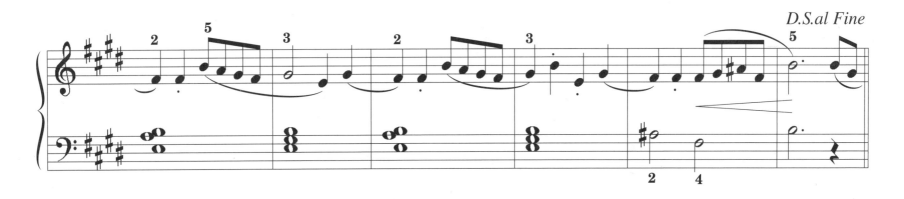

Two and Three-note Slurs

Barcarolle

from *The Tales of Hoffmann*

19/20

Moderato

J. Offenbach

Be sure to observe the two and three-note slurs. When they are played correctly, they will imitate the rocking motion of a gondola as it glides over the waters of a Venetian canal.

Short and Long Slurs
The Cuckoo Clock

21/22

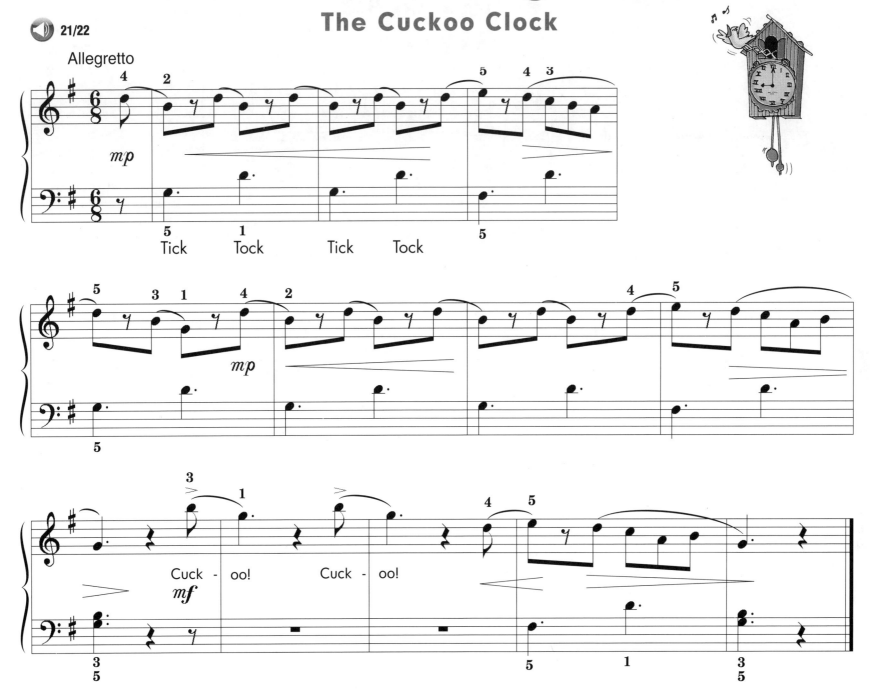

Staccato Thirds
The Overland Stage

🔊 **23/24**

Sostenuto is a musical term meaning 'in a sustained manner.' It is indicated by a little line placed above or below a note, like this:

♩ or 𝅗𝅥

In the following piece, see how much contrast you can make between the chords marked **staccato** and those with the **sostenuto** sign.

Allegretto

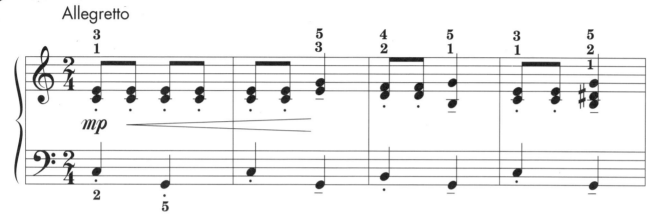

Work Sheet New Key – A♭ Major

A FLAT MAJOR has four flats – B♭ E♭ A♭ D♭.

Write the A flat major scale, using accidentals as necessary to preserve the scale pattern. Remember that half steps occur only between the **3rd and 4th** and **7th and 8th** degrees of the scale. All others are whole steps.

Broken Chord Study
in A Flat Major

TEACHER'S NOTE: While the art of pedalling has not yet been covered (it will be given in detail later in the course) it seems advisable to allow its use in simple, elementary form in this piece as well as in some others which follow, especially as extended arpeggio passages are rather lifeless without it. At this point simply explain to the student that the damper (right) pedal is pressed down at the word 'Ped.' and is held until the asterisk (*) appears, when it is immediately released.

Giant Redwood Trees

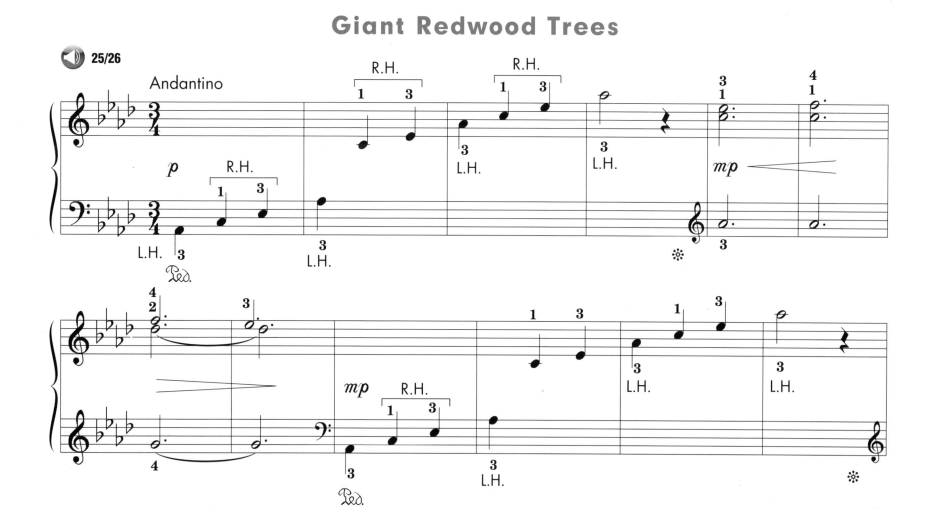

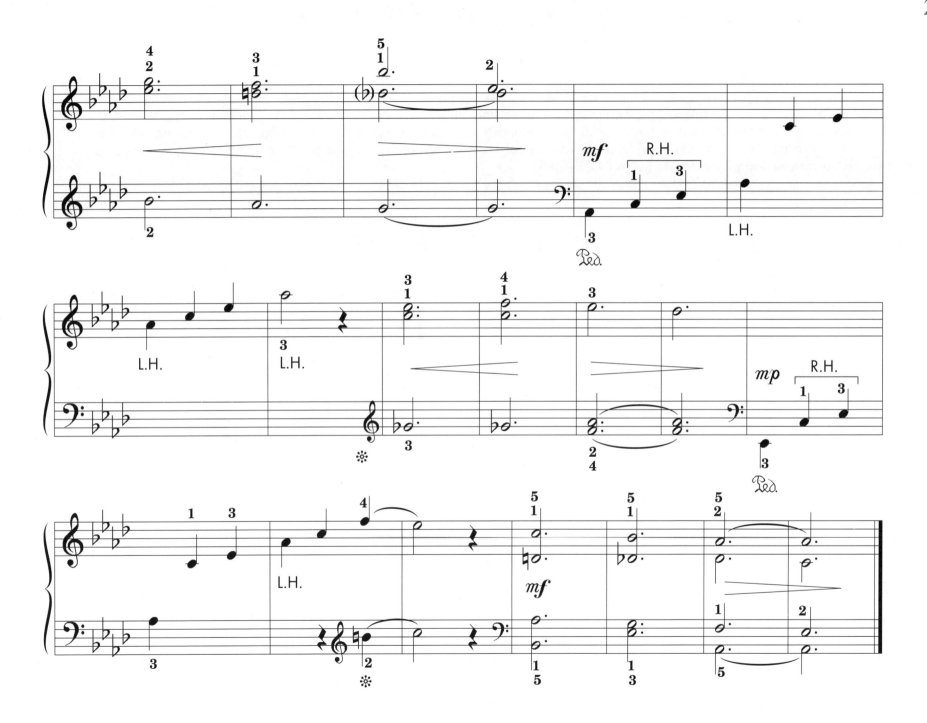

Staccato Study

TEACHER'S NOTE: The following piece may be played with either wrist or finger staccato. If wrist staccato is used, the repeated notes are played with the same finger. If finger staccato is used, it calls for a change of finger on each note. For this reason, two sets of fingering are given. For full descriptions of the various staccato touches (finger, wrist and forearm) see John Thompson's HANON STUDIES.

From
The Opera *William Tell*

27/28

G. Rossini

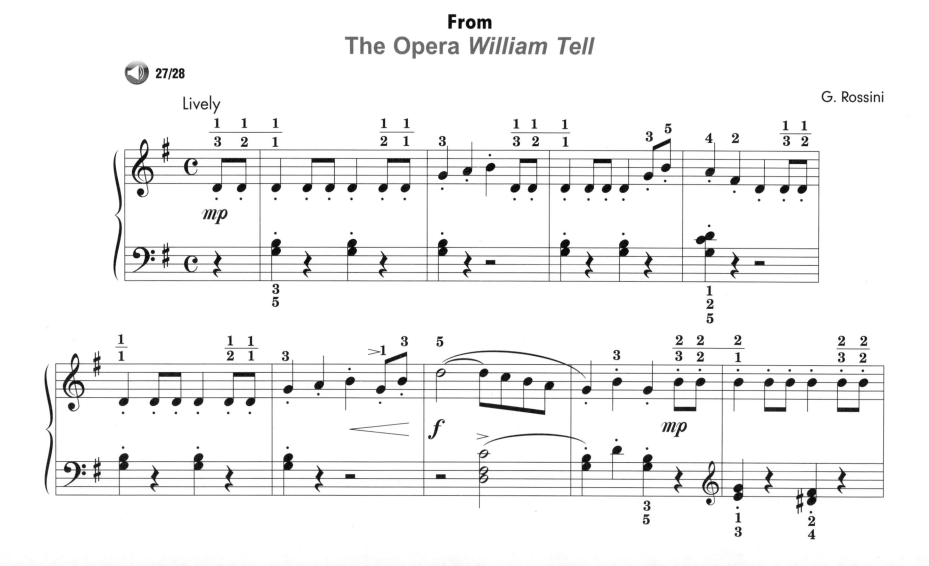

From
The Beautiful Blue Danube

29/30

Moderato

Johann Strauss

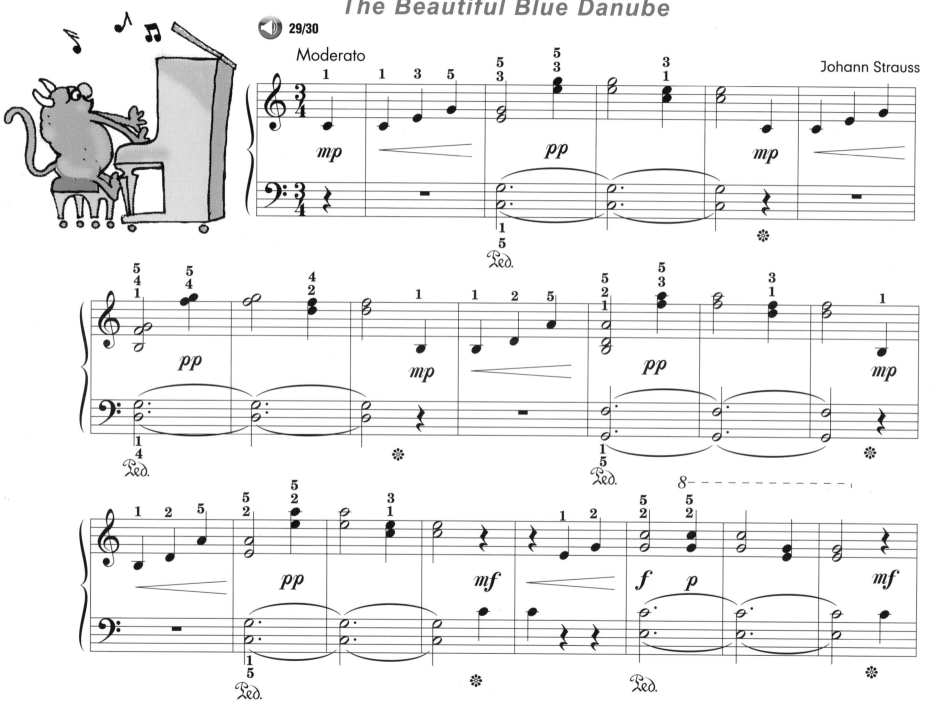

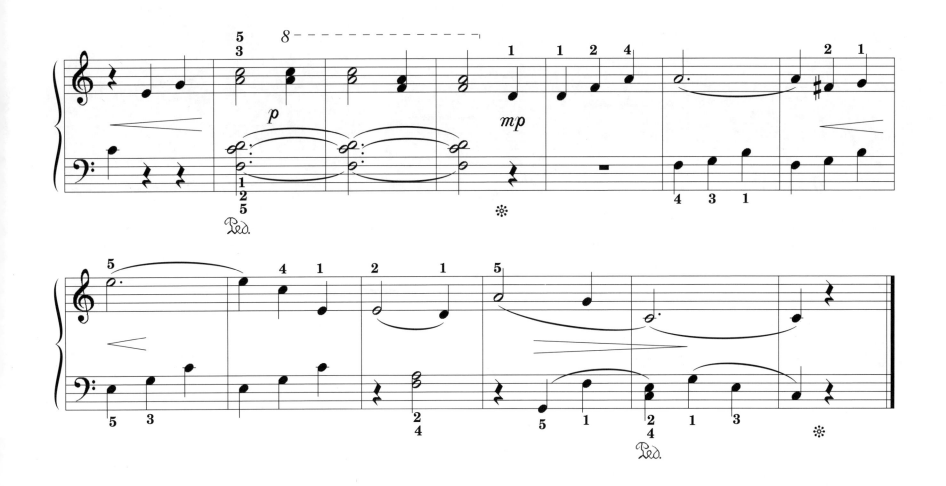

Cross-Hand Piece
Scampering Squirrels

31/32

Allegro

Syncopation
College Capers

To produce a syncopated effect, be sure to apply heavy accents as marked.

33/34

Allegro moderato

30

Work Sheet New Key – B Major

B MAJOR has five sharps – F♯ C♯ G♯ D♯ A♯.

Write the B major scale, using accidentals as necessary to preserve the scale pattern. Remember that half steps occur only between the **3rd and 4th** and **7th and 8th** degrees of the scale. All others are whole steps.

Study in B Major

Bohemian Dance

Song of Twilight

Nocturne

37/38

NOCTURNE means night piece. It is a title often used for compositions that are lyric with a mood suggesting the quiet of the evening.

Andantino

Staccato and Sostenuto

From "Hopak"

39/40

Play this dance with plenty of fire and dash. Apply sharp staccatos, heavy accents and watch for the occasional **sostenuto** marks.

Allegro

Modest P. Moussorgsky

Work Sheet New Key – D♭ Major

D FLAT MAJOR has five flats – B♭ E♭ A♭ D♭ G♭.

Write the D flat major scale, using accidentals as necessary to preserve the scale pattern. Remember that half steps occur only between the **3rd and 4th** and **7th and 8th** degrees of the scale. All others are whole steps.

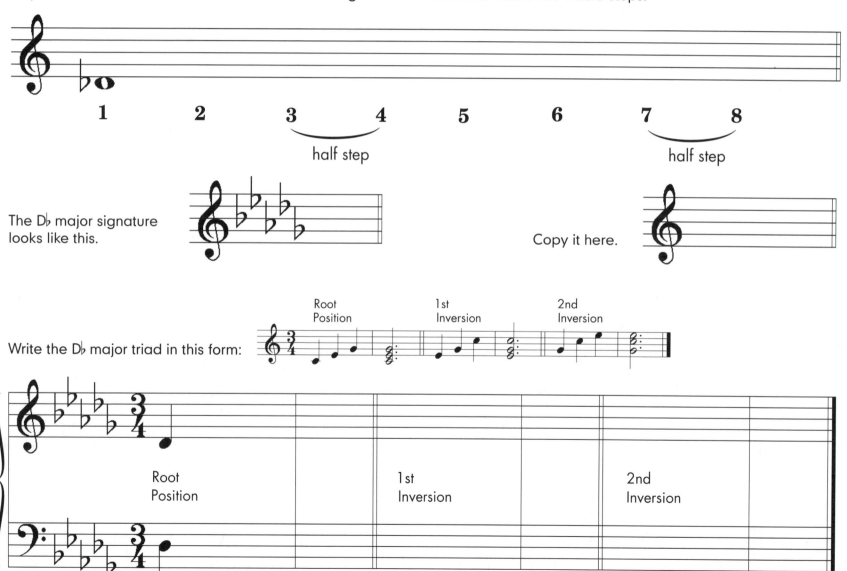

Etude in D Flat Major

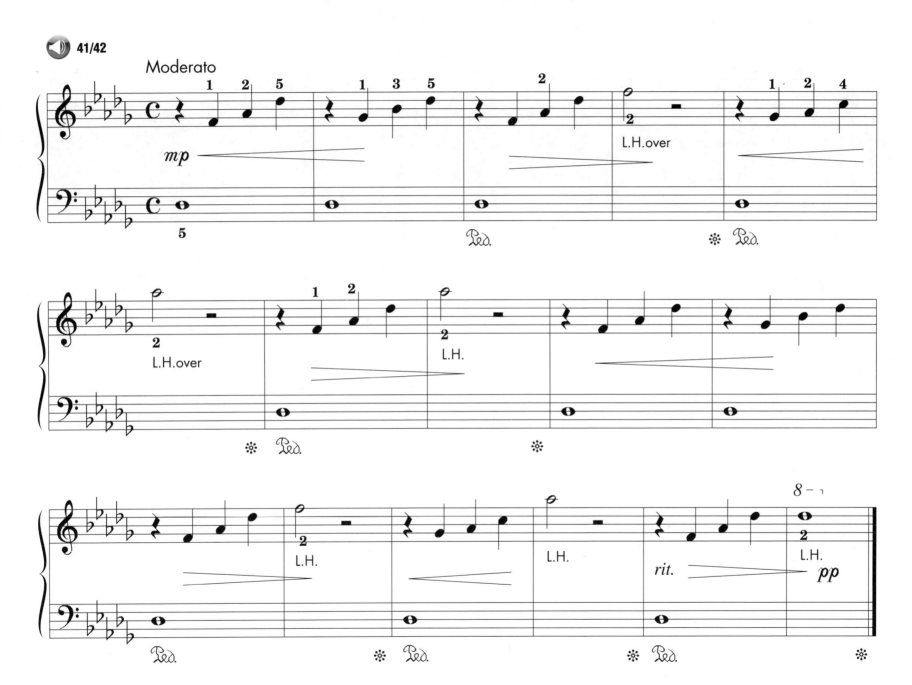

At the Skating Rink

Moderato

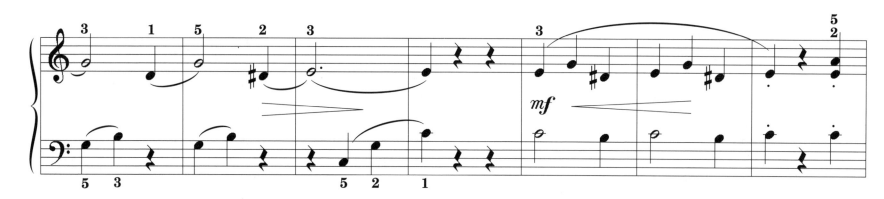

Work Sheet New Key – G♭ Major

G FLAT MAJOR has six flats – B♭ E♭ A♭ D♭ G♭ C♭.

Write the G flat major scale, using accidentals as necessary to preserve the scale pattern. Remember that half steps occur only between the **3rd and 4th** and **7th and 8th** degrees of the scale. All others are whole steps.

Study in G Flat Major
Korean Serenade

Watch for the new flat (C♭). It occurs only once. Be sure to find it!

45/46   Moderato

The Man on the Flying Trapeze

47/48

Moderato

Walter O'Keefe

From
"Narcissus"

Ethelbert Nevin

49/50

44

New Scales and Chords

45

Ab Major

Db Major

Gb Major

E Major

46

B Major

F# Major

C# Major

Glossary
of musical terms and expression marks used

⟩ (Accent)	… special emphasis on a note or chord		*mf* – **Mezzo Forte**	… moderately loud
Allegretto	… light and lively		*mp* – **Mezzo Piano**	… moderately soft
Allegro	… fast		**Moderato**	… moderately fast
Andante	… slow		⌢ **Pause**	… hold the note or chord longer according to taste
Andantino	… slow, but not as slow as andante		*pp* – **Pianissimo**	… very soft
Animato	… animated		*p* – **Piano**	… soft
a tempo	… return to original speed		**Poco**	… little
⟨ – **Crescendo**	… gradually louder		:‖	… repeat sign
⟩ – **Decrescendo**	… gradually softer		**R.H.**	… right hand
Diminuendo	… softer by degrees		**Rit./Ritard.**	… slower by degrees
f – **Forte**	… loud		⌢ **Slur**	… connected
ff – **Fortissimo**	… very loud		**Staccato**	… detached, short
Legato	… smooth and connected		**Tempo**	… rate of speed
L.H.	… left hand		**Vivace**	… fast and vivacious
8ᵛᵃ	… play one octave higher			

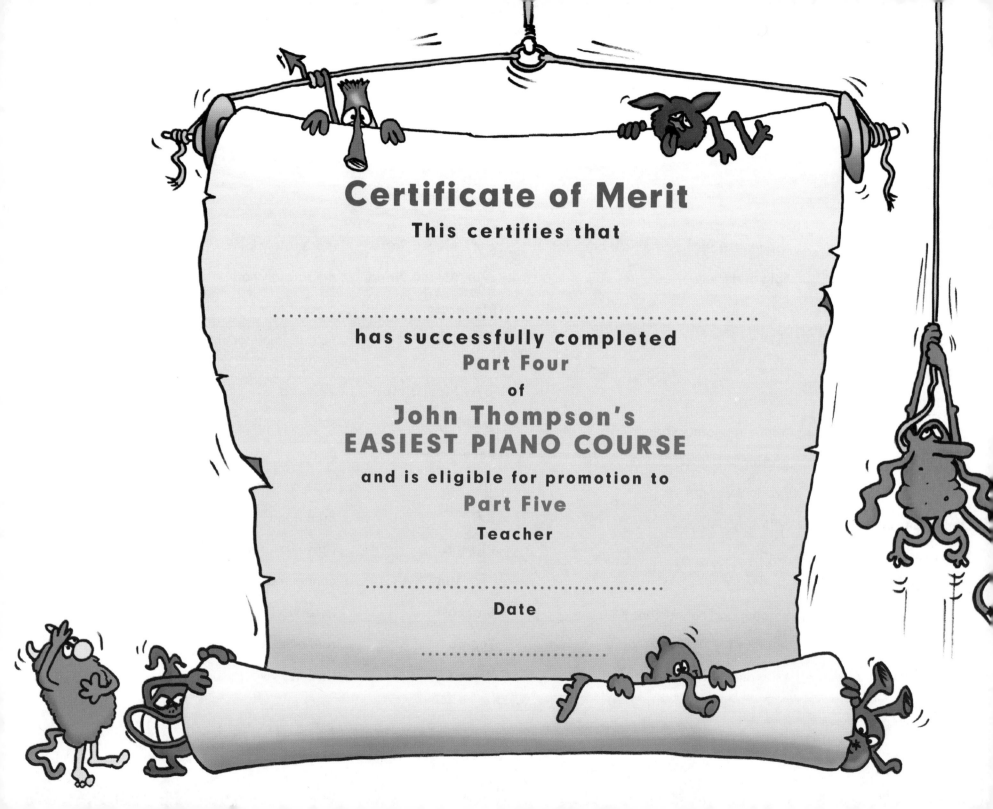

Certificate of Merit

This certifies that

....

has successfully completed
Part Four
of
John Thompson's
EASIEST PIANO COURSE
and is eligible for promotion to
Part Five

Teacher

....

Date

....